THEN & NOW®

MILL VALLEY

OPPOSITE: Mill Valley visitors are seen here striding across Miller Avenue in their hiking outfits, no doubt on their way to an outing on Mount Tamalpais. The photograph, taken in the mid-1930s, is captioned "Hundreds of hikers each week-end roam the picturesque hills and woods surrounding Mill Valley, Calif." The train station is crowded with people, and up at the corner, on Throckmorton Avenue, a number of other tourists can be seen walking toward the hiking trails or perhaps the beaches at Stinson or Muir Beach. Behind the train depot, the Mount Tamalpais Scenic Railway took visitors on an exciting ride to the top of the mountain. (Courtesy of Mill Valley Library History Room [MVLHR].)

THEN & NOW®

MILL VALLEY

Suki Hill

For my town, my home, Mill Valley. There is no place that I would rather be.

Copyright © 2007 by Suki Hill
ISBN 978-0-7385-5574-4

Library of Congress Control Number: 2007930845

Published by Arcadia Publishing
Charleston, South Carolina

Printed in the United States of America

Then and Now is a registered trademark and is used under license from
Salamander Books Limited

For all general information contact Arcadia Publishing at:
Telephone 843-853-2070
Fax 843-853-0044
E-mail sales@arcadiapublishing.com
For customer service and orders:
Toll-Free 1-888-313-2665

Visit us on the Internet at www.arcadiapublishing.com

ON THE FRONT COVER: Throckmorton Avenue is shown in 1929, the year the art-deco Sequoia Theater opened its doors with the promise to soon have "the talking device." The office of Pacific Gas and Electric can be seen on the left. On the far right is the Purity Market—the first chain grocery store in Mill Valley. The next building up was a livery stable, and beyond that is the building that housed Sonapa Farms in the 1950s and is currently Champagne French Café. In 2007, the Sequoia Theater still stands, having survived a roof collapse in 2005. The theater has undergone a number of renovations, including being split into two screening rooms. It has nevertheless retained its charming art-deco exterior and hosts the very popular Mill Valley Film Festival. Boys on "razor scooters," all the rage, cross the street. The Banana Republic is on the far right corner of the street. (Then courtesy of MVLHR; now courtesy of Suki Hill.)

ON THE BACK COVER: Residents of Mill Valley, including women, men, children, and a dog, are seen in this picture, taken *c.* 1896. The sign on the building says, "Mill Valley House," "Mill Valley Restaurant," "Palace Ice Cream & Lunch Parlors," and the three hard-to-read signs say, "Report," "Ice," and "Examiner." The location of this building was about 38 Miller Avenue, now Mill Creek Plaza, and before that "Old Brown's Furniture Store." All the men wear hats except one, probably the owner, and the woman next to him with a blanket draped over her lap is probably his wife. (Courtesy of Mill Valley Library History Room.)

CONTENTS

ACKNOWLEDGMENTS

The author wishes to thank a number of people who helped in this endeavor. Allison Wisnom, who first introduced me to Arcadia, was a last-minute godsend, helping organize the photographs and the captions and generally keeping me focused on what I found to be the difficult part of doing this book. Chuck Oldenburg, a real historian and devoted member of the Homestead Valley community, was a great support, and we had rather a lot of fun exploring his neck of the woods. I learned a great deal from him and wish I could have used more photographs. Other members of the Mill Valley Historical Society were also very supportive, notably Bill Devlin, who furnished me with all his father's pictures of Mill Valley from the 1960s and tried to help with historical facts and references. Allen Testa, a librarian at the Mill Valley Library, cheerfully provided me with scans of historical photographs when they were available. Jim Staley very kindly gave me the use of many of his vintage Mill Valley postcards. John Poultney, my editor, offered enthusiastic support. Rhonda Dubin, who has always helped me in so many ways, provided the final editing talent and helped me finish the project. Claudine Chalmers's book, *Early Mill Valley*, was a great help, as was Barry Spitz's meticulously researched book, *Mill Valley: The Early Years*.

(Please note that courtesy lines for the Mill Valley Library History Room are abbreviated to MVLHR. "Courtesy of Suki Hill" designations are, with obvious exceptions of very old photographs from her collection, assigned to photographs taken by the author.)

INTRODUCTION

Mill Valley has likely always been something of an Eden. Early settlers reported abundant wild game, vast meadowlands of shoulder-high grasses, creeks filled with salmon, and the surrounding mountainsides covered with pine nuts and acorns as well as glorious stands of redwood and oak. Today Mill Valley has become a real estate Eden. Its physical charm, its proximity to Muir Woods, the Pacific Ocean, and San Francisco, and the beauty of the surrounding rolling hills have made the town one of the most desirable places to live in the nation. The town's most prominent feature is its beautiful Mount Tamalpais, the "Sleeping Lady." Mill Valley has certainly undergone enormous changes in the past 100 years. After the Golden Gate Bridge opened in 1937, Mill Valley became more accessible to San Francisco, resulting in a mini real estate boom. To this day, real estate is a principal business in the town. Early 20th-century prices advertised one-acre lots for $250. As of July 2006, the median price for a house was $1,258,900. In spite of all this, the town retains an old-world charm and a welcoming spirit. What might be seen as a disparate community of graying "hippies" and new "dot-comers" is kept together by their mutual affection for this truly livable place. This is no "bedroom community." There is an award-winning library, an active historical society, a civic-minded Outdoor Art Club, a renovated city hall, excellent fire and police services in a Public Safety Building that opened 20 years ago, and a beautiful community center. There is a wonderful absence of franchise businesses in town, and shopping here is a pleasurable experience with friendly personal service. The plaza, in the center of town, is an appealing gathering place for residents and tourists alike.

Styles come and go, but the spirit of the town has always been vibrant. Each generation has used mountain, marshland, and valley in its own fashion, for sport, celebration, or worship. Mount Tamalpais has always been the defining, exhilarating presence that has bound its residents into a wonderful community in a truly fine and welcoming place.

CHAPTER 1

PERSPECTIVE AND VIEWS

A rare dusting of snow is seen here on the peaks of Mount Tamalpais. The beautiful and serene "Sleeping Lady" has always been the main attraction for visitors. People have come to Mill Valley to hike, to picnic, to run the Dipsea race, to ride the mountain railway, and to build homes. All of these activities have centered on Mount Tamalpais. And nearby, on the other side of Panoramic Ridge, one can commune with giant stands of redwoods in Muir Woods or visit two beautiful beaches on the Pacific Ocean. In this chapter, there are a number of views of Mill Valley—the entryways from both the north and the south, overlooks to Homestead Valley, Mill Valley itself, and other neighborhoods—to show the interesting changes that have taken place. It should be noted that because of the enormous growth of trees and hedges and the proliferation of fences, it was difficult to portray some of the current views of Mill Valley. (Courtesy of Suki Hill.)

This picture postcard was taken of Mill Valley in November 1913, almost 100 years ago. One can find the train station slightly to the right of center and clearly see many of the principal streets of the town. East Blithedale Avenue goes off to the right, and Lovell is in the foreground. In attempting to find the same vantage point, the author discovered the image was taken approximately from her home on the east side off Panoramic Ridge. Mount Carmel Church's roof and steeple are visible, as are East Blithedale and several homes on Summit Avenue. (Then courtesy of Jim Staley; now courtesy of Suki Hill.)

Both photographs were taken from the same exact spot, a deck at 122 Mountain Lane, a delightful cabin on the east side of Panoramic Ridge. This particular parcel of land, like many others in Mill Valley, was purchased for the price of a subscription to the *Chronicle/Examiner* newspaper in the early 1920s. The photograph with the spindly redwoods was taken about 1925. By 1975, those trees had grown enormous, blocking the view of Mount Tamalpais. They are seen here being topped by the owner of the cabin. (Both courtesy of Suki Hill.)

This view of Mill Valley, taken from what is now the top of Summit Avenue, was made around the beginning of the 20th century. Miller Avenue and Blithedale Avenue are the prominent roads that can be clearly seen. Both meet up with State Highway 101 (today's Camino Alto), evident across the center of the picture. Left of center is the virgin Strawberry Peninsula, and beyond is Angel Island and the East Bay. San Francisco is in the background. The marshlands of Mill Valley can also be seen. In the 2007 photograph with the identical view, the bridge over Richardson Bay, built in 1931, is evident. Strawberry and Sausalito are completely developed, and Mill Valley is not to be seen because of the tremendous growth of trees. (Then courtesy of Mill Valley Library History Room; now courtesy of Suki Hill.)

PERSPECTIVE AND VIEWS

The view of Homestead Valley is part of a panoramic photograph taken around the dawn of the 20th century, and it shows the old Homestead Hall. The area was primarily dairy farms at this time, and houses were widely separated on fairly large tracts of land. This photograph was taken from nearly the same vantage point, but because of tremendous tree growth, the numerous houses that have sprung up are barely visible. (Both courtesy of Chuck Oldenburg.)

This view of a portion of the Locust district of Mill Valley was taken from Ethel Avenue in the early 1930s. There are a number of cars parked along the railroad tracks, as this was a train stop. One can see the Efficie Garage with gas pumps out front. This building has been replaced by a 7/11 store. Across the street, where the Mill Valley Coffee Shop is now, there appears to be a candy and soda fountain. (Then courtesy of Jim Staley; now courtesy of Suki Hill.)

Locust District
Mill Valley, Calif.

A family poses on upper Throckmorton Avenue around 1890. There are no homes to be seen, the road is unpaved, and the scenery is quite beautiful, with Mount Tamalpais in the background. One hundred and seventeen years later, the same view shows a paved street and a very developed neighborhood. Some turn-of-the-20th-century homes still stand, but they are obscured by tall trees and hedges. (Then courtesy of MVLHR; now courtesy of Suki Hill.)

The notable difference between the two views of Tam Junction (in 1966 and 2007, 41 years later) is the large development on the hill in the background, the increase in traffic (a constant in Mill Valley today), and the usual growth of trees, making everything seem a little bit more attractive. Tam Junction is still a very busy intersection and the gateway for tourists who wish to travel to Muir Woods, Stinson Beach, and Muir Beach. (Both courtesy of Suki Hill.)

PERSPECTIVE AND VIEWS

This 2007 photograph shows the old Fireside Motel in the center surrounded by 50 units being built as part of the area's state-mandated quota of affordable housing. The Fireside has been a landmark to the entrance to Tam Junction and Mill Valley for 50 years. In this photograph, taken in the late 1940s, one can see the Fireside in all its original splendor. (Then courtesy of Jim Staley; now courtesy of Suki Hill.)

This amazing photograph of the road and train tracks into Mill Valley was taken in 1898. This 2007 shot is taken from roughly the same vantage point, but only the mountain is recognizable. The overpass is part of Highway 101, and the cars are heading north. The cars traveling underneath the overpass are headed to Tam Junction, Highway 1, or Miller Avenue. (Then courtesy of MVLHR; now courtesy of Suki Hill.)

Courtesy of the Lucretia Little History Room, Mill Valley Public Library

This *c.* 1900 image of Miller Avenue shows the Jacob Gardner house prominently on the left side of the photograph; the structure was highly visible when people approached the town by train or along the as-yet-unpaved road. Miller Avenue is still one of two main roads into town but has been considerably widened with a median strip planted with trees. The Gardner house still stands, but is no longer visible from this vantage point. (Then courtesy of MVLHR; now courtesy of Suki Hill.)

Taken in 1931, this view of Highway 101 looks south toward San Francisco. This is also known as the Tiburon Wye. The sign directed traffic west and to San Francisco, connecting motorists to the old road to Sausalito. There was no bridge over Richardson Bay, and the Golden Gate Bridge had not yet been built. People were ferried back and forth to San Francisco. On the left is the road to Tiburon. The near right building is Avilla's Richfield Gas Station. Currently there is a Richfield Arco Station further down the road. Across the road was a large dairy, and cows grazed on the hill above. No longer a hill for grazing, the area is now a large development of houses, built in the 1950s, and this hillside is called Enchanted Knolls. Highway 101 has become a major four-lane freeway, and the exit to Mill Valley and Tiburon is in the process of being widened to accommodate the enormous increase in traffic. (Then courtesy of MVLHR; now courtesy of Suki Hill.)

CHAPTER 2

HOMES AND
NEIGHBORHOODS

As a sentinal, Mt. Tamalpais towers above the City of Mill Valley, Calif.

The real estate market phrase "location, location, location" says it all about Mill Valley. The town is on everyone's lips. It's the place to be. Since the 1940s and 1950s, real estate has become a major business in Mill Valley. Areas like Sycamore Park, which were slightly dull in the 1950s, have been "upgraded," landscaped, and generally made very appealing and attractive. Modest-sized homes in all neighborhoods have been torn down and replaced with 4,000–5,000-square-foot mini mansions. This view of the Sycamore Park area of Mill Valley was taken in 1944, probably from the hill above, once a dairy and now the Enchanted Knolls subdivision. The street in the foreground is Amicita Avenue, to the left is Juanita Avenue, and on the right is East Blithedale Avenue. John Reed was the first white settler and landowner in Mill Valley. Within the Sycamore Park triangle, John Reed began to build his adobe house at approximately La Goma Street and Locke Lane between 1835 and 1837. A landing on a nearby slough (the marshlands have long since been filled in) provided easy access to his home and large rancho, a Spanish land grant. (Courtesy of Jim Staley.)

Looking toward downtown Mill Valley on Miller Avenue in the 1940s, one can see a dry cleaners, a soda fountain shop, and, farther down, the Efficient Garage and Chrysler dealership, now a 7/11 store in 2007. (Then courtesy of Jim Staley; now courtesy of Suki Hill.)

This home is in the Tamalpais Park neighborhood and still stands today. It is now adjacent to the parking lot used by customers of the Mill Valley Services. In the photograph taken in 1922, two ladies stand on the snowy lawn, though snow was an unusual occurrence in Mill Valley. The craftsman-style bungalow was built in 1909 by John Forbes, a cabinet maker who had his business in San Francisco. (Then courtesy of Chuck Oldenburg; now courtesy of Suki Hill.)

The large, brown-shingle house pictured around 1907 belonged to Alfred and Fannie Worley. In 1909, some 20 acres of the Worley tract property were subdivided south of LaVerne Avenue into 68 lots on Ferndale and Melrose Streets. The original house at 235 LaVerne burned down in 1940 and was replaced by a small stucco house, which was demolished in 2000 and replaced by this 4,000-square-foot modern-day residence made almost entirely of steel. (Then courtesy of Chuck Oldenburg; now courtesy of Suki Hill.)

This photograph was taken in 1922 during an unusual snowstorm that hit the town of Mill Valley and dumped several feet of snow on Mount Tamalpais. The image reveals railroad tracks in the foreground of what is now Miller Avenue. Today the home at 254 Miller Avenue still stands; it is barely visible, as the trees and high hedges have grown significantly. (Then courtesy of Chuck Oldenburg; now courtesy of Suki Hill.)

This photograph shows Joaquin Silva, who built the home at 304 LaVerne Avenue (note the saw in hand), with his wife, Mary, and daughter Sirniana standing on the steps of their home around 1925. The house remained in this location until 2000, when it was demolished and replaced by a much larger home that is featured in the second photograph. The contractor for this new home, Nicole Scholvinck, is also the owner, along with her husband, Mark. They are pictured here with their two children. (Both courtesy of Suki Hill.)

HOMES AND NEIGHBORHOODS

Lillian Ferguson built a weekend retreat in 1907 on her property in an area known as "Three Groves." One of the three groves of trees was a beautiful stand of redwoods. This is a piture of her deck at her home on Montford Avenue, taken around 1925. Three Groves was sold to George Sandy in 1930. He built dams on the creek to create a lake and a swimming pool, and brought in sand from Carmel to make a beach on the lake. In 1979, one third of the property was purchased by the Nielsen family. The house and garden have been carefully restored and improved upon. Shelia Nielsen is pictured in 1007 on the deck. (Then courtesy of Sheila Nielsen; now courtesy of Suki Hill.)

Mary Silva Libori and her husband, Frank, stand in front of a picket fence at 260 LaVerne Street. This photograph was taken around 1925. The couple divorced, and Mary and her two children moved back in with her parents at 304 LaVerne Street. The house remained intact until 2001, when a second story was added. A white picket fence is still a feature of this sweet little house. (Both courtesy of Suki Hill.)

This charming house was built by Alexander Eells on his eight-acre property. This photograph was taken around 1910. The property was situated between Montford and LaVerne Streets on both sides of Reed Creek. The original house still stands at 424 LaVerne Street, although it cannot be seen from the same angle, as the trees have grown significantly. (Then courtesy of Chuck Oldenburg; now courtesy of Suki Hill.)

In 1893, Alonzo Coffin built this house, nicknamed the "Ferryboat House" for its resemblance to the ferry boats plying the San Francisco Bay. This side view of the landmark home was taken in 1913. The 2007 photograph shows a view of the house from the front, with Melanie Palmer standing in the foreground. The Palmer family has owned this house since 1963, and one can see that it has been beautifully maintained and preserved. (Then courtesy of Melanie Palmer; now courtesy of Suki Hill.)

In the early 1900s, the Millwood train station stop was moved one block south to Locust Avenue and was renamed the Locust Avenue Station. Today in this approximate place is a 7-11 store, and the mountain is still visible in the background. There are no longer train tracks that run down Miller Avenue; instead there is a two-lane road on each side separated by a median with planted trees. (Then courtesy of Jim Staley; now courtesy of Suki Hill.)

This is a *c.* 1970 side view of the famous Gardner villa at 239 Miller Avenue. By the 1970s, the house had fallen into disrepair but was happily inhabited by four elderly people. They shared the kitchen and basically formed their own retirement community. When the house was sold in the early 1990s, the rooms became professional offices and remain that way today. (Both courtesy of Suki Hill.)

HOMES AND NEIGHBORHOODS

This photograph is the front of a postcard that was sent from Mill Valley on August 7, 1911, from a mother to her son in Stockton, California. The stamp on this postcard cost 1¢. This picture shows some beautiful homes above and on Bigelow Avenue. The street is unpaved and virtually treeless. Today just hints of the homes still standing can be seen as the street has become so lush with greenery. Nevertheless, a number of the homes shown in the postcard still stand. (Then courtesy of Jim Staley; now courtesy of Suki Hill.)

Bigelow Avenue, Mill Valley, Cal.

At the intersection of Buena Vista Avenue and Hill Street, a girl in tights and a tutu crosses the street with her brother and their dog on a leash. Above, Buena Vista Avenue is Oakdale Avenue. A number of homes still stand and can be identified from the original photograph. In these photographs, 49 Buena Vista Avenue can be identified, as well as 59 Buena Vista Avenue. (Then courtesy of Jim Staley; now courtesy of Suki Hill.)

Sunny Heights, Mill Valley, Cal.

HOMES AND NEIGHBORHOODS

CHAPTER

BUSINESSES

The Mill Valley Lumber Company as it appeared in 1991 looks very much the same as it did 100 years ago. It began as the Dollar Lumber Company, and some of its first structures are still in use and are some of Mill Valley's oldest. Although it has changed hands several times, the business is arguably the oldest one in the same location in the town. Mill Valley was a fast-growing town after about 1900. The company has always furnished the necessary lumber for the building of its homes and businesses, as it continues to do today. Tom Cerri and his two sons, Danny and Tony, bought the business from Jim Merchant and the property from John Castleman in 1998 and have made very few changes—hence the business continues to thrive, with the lumberyard supplying local contractors as well as residents. (Courtesy of Suki Hill.)

Throckmorton Avenue is shown in 1929, the year the art-deco Sequoia Theater opened its doors with the promise to soon have "the talking device." The office of Pacific Gas and Electric can be seen on the left. On the far right is the Purity Market, the first chain grocery store in Mill Valley. The next building up was a livery stable, and beyond that was the building that housed Sonapa Farms in the 1950s and is currently Champagne French Café. In 2007, the Sequoia Theater still stands, having survived a roof collapse in 2005. The theater has undergone a number of renovations, including being split into two screening rooms, but has retained its very charming art-deco style and is the central location for the very popular Mill Valley Film Festival. Boys on "razor scooters," all the rage, cross the street. The Banana Republic is on the far right corner of the street. (Then courtesy of MVLHR; now courtesy of Suki Hill.)

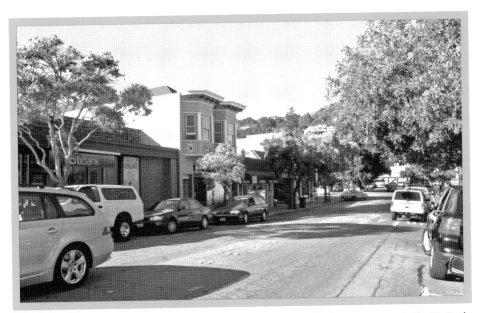

Next to the original Mill Valley Market (its sign is prominent on the side of the building with the Coca-Cola sign) is Northwestern Savings, advertising an interest rate of three percent in the late 1940s. Today this spot is occupied by CitiBank, whose interest rates in 2007 are comparable—about three percent! (Then courtesy of Jim Staley; now courtesy of Suki Hill.)

The Mill Valley Lumber Company began as the Dollar Lumber Company in 1892. The yard furnished boards, shingles, posts, shakes, sidings, moldings, cabinets, and the like to the growing town. Here, in 1991, one hundred years later, is the owner, Jim Merchant, with some of the yard workers. Still an important business in the community, the company was purchased by the Cerri family in 1998; they pose in 2007 with yard workers. (Both courtesy of Suki Hill.)

40

Built in 1915, the Hub Theater was a movie theater showing silent films. It was once at the heart of Mill Valley's artistic life. When the Sequoia Theater announced in 1929 that it would soon be having the "talking device," the Hub became passé and went into rapid decline. Over the years, it has gone through many changes and had several different uses. In 1999, Lucy Mercer bought the building and began a meticulous and handsome renovation of the old theater. It is once again a lively, vibrant venue for live music, dance, theater, comedy, and fine art. This photograph was taken in 2007 with Lucy front and center and some members of the theater's enthusiastic staff. (Then courtesy of MVLHR; now courtesy of Suki Hill.)

Graham's Garage at 202 Almonte Boulevard was founded in 1929 by Charles Graham. His son, Charles S. Graham Jr., pictured here with his assistant Steve, was described in his obituary in 1991 as a "master mechanic and machinist." He died at the age of 82 and was much respected and adored by his customers and members of the community. The building at 202 Almonte Boulevard currently houses a candle-making business. The owner poses here for a picture in front of the building in 2007. (Both courtesy of Suki Hill.)

118 Throckmorton Avenue now houses the Mill Valley Hat Box. Next door, at 116 Throckmorton, is Lando Mill Valley, a women's clothing store. Down the street, one has a glimpse of CitiBank. The address 120 Throckmorton was the original location of the Mill Valley Market. The family dates their business as having officially opened on July 4, 1929. Frank Canepa and his wife, Kathe, lived upstairs. This photograph was taken by Jim Canepa, the son, around 1950. The old car parked in from was Jim's mode of transportation when he was around 16 years old. (Then courtesy of MVLHR; now courtesy of Suki Hill.)

The photograph of Jenny Low (front and center) and some of her staff was made in 2000. Jenny Low's is located at 38 Miller Avenue and has been in this location for more than 20 years. The restaurant is scheduled to close before the end of the year 2007. The *c.* 1890 Mill Valley House stood at 28–30 Miller Avenue, approximately the same location. The vintage photograph shows a large number of people posing in front of the building. They are presumably residents of the hotel, employees, children, and a dog. Within the hotel are the Palace Ice Cream and Lunch Parlors and the Mill Valley Restaurant. They sold ice and the *Examiner*, and there is a sign that says "Report For Sale Here." All the men wear hats except one, probably the owner, and the woman next to him with a blanket draped over her lap is probably his wife. (Then courtesy of MVLHR; now courtesy of Suki Hill.)

Originally the Miller Avenue Shopping Center, "The Quonsets," as this building was known to the locals, opened in 1947. The business eventually became Jerry's Meats and Delicatessen, as well as a pharmacy. Jerry Carver, his wife and daughter, and two employees are pictured here in 1979. In 1994, Whole Foods took over the building; many of the employees (and one small daughter), as well as the manager, are pictured here in this photograph taken in 1998. (Both courtesy of Suki Hill.)

The Quality Market was located at 14 Corte Madera Avenue until the 1940s, when it became the Green Frog Grocery. This picture dates from around 1920 and shows presumably the owners of the store. In 1987, some of the staff are posing in front of the same building, now the Mill Valley Market. Owners Jim and Bob Canepa are the two men at top left. Jim's two sons Dave and Doug are the two men on the far right. (Then courtesy of MVLHR; now courtesy of Suki Hill.)

The train to Mount Tamalpais passed to the right of the Brabo Building, pictured here about 1925. At this time, it was occupied by Marin Milk Company, Egger Real Estate, and a tailor, J. M. Jones. The train tracks for the Mount Tamalpais Scenic Railway were removed in 1930, and a building was constructed in the empty passageway. The building is currently occupied by the Pleasure Principle, the oldest proprietorship in Mill Valley. Next door is a women's clothing store, Cavallos. From 1939 to 1980, it was Rutherford's Drugstore, an institution in Mill Valley. (Then courtesy of MVLHR; now courtesy of Suki Hill.)

Jack Hansen, proprietor of the Louvre, so named because of the artwork that hung above the bar, poses here in the foreground with his brothers and son around 1901. This saloon, one of four in the area known as "Jagtown," was located on East Blithedale Avenue and Grove Street. This apparently rather serious drinking establishment and its building no longer exist. Shown is a photograph of the young woman bartender at Vasco's, taken in 2006, an upscale bar and restaurant at the corner of Throckmorton Avenue and Bernard Street. Originally the Old Mill Tavern, it closed in 1981 and has gone through a series of different restaurant businesses. (Then courtesy of MVLHR; now courtesy of Suki Hill.)

This *c.* 1918 photograph shows the busy street life along Miller Avenue looking toward Throckmorton Avenue and Lytton Square. At least one hiker with a backpack can be seen striding through town. A dapper young gentleman stands posing in the middle of the picture, and people around him appear to be busily running errands. The car in the foreground looks like a 1915 Model T couplet. In the 2007 shot, cars dominate the same scene. A young woman confers with someone through a car window, and a few people can be seen on the sidewalk of a still very busy street. (Then courtesy of MVLHR; now courtesy of Suki Hill.)

Greyhound buses took over the train depot in 1940. This picture, taken in the early 1950s, show Brun Liebes at the counter of the Greyhound Bus Station, waiting on Mrs. Melvin Klyce and her two daughters. Then, in the 1980s, the City of Mill Valley began an improvement program that, among other things, sanctioned the remodeling of the city-owned depot; it became the Depot Bookstore and Café. In the 2007 photograph, a customer is waited on in the identical location depicted in the 1950s photograph. (Then courtesy of MVLHR; now courtesy of Suki Hill.)

Here we see the Keystone Building on the north side of Lytton Square. The building was built in 1906 and remodeled in the Tudor style in 1934. The square is looking quite bleak with only small saplings in this 1967 photograph. The redwood tree in the center is still quite small. As one can see in the same view today, the trees now obscure much of the building. Suffice it to say that Lytton Square and the Plaza across the street function as the true hub of Mill Valley. (Then courtesy of Madison Devlin; now courtesy of Suki Hill.)

This is the Mill Valley Market in the 1960s, before it expanded into the space occupied by Pohli Real Estate and the Pet Salon in 1966. In 1976, it further expanded into Quinn's Bar and the White Mill Restaurant. It is photographed here in 2007 with a new look but is barely seen through the trees. This award-winning, community-minded business is the only independently operated market in Mill Valley and one of the few remaining in Marin County. (Then courtesy of Madison Devlin; now courtesy of Suki Hill.)

Pictured here in 1985 are some of the staff of Smith and Hawken as well as the resident cat. The location of the flagship store was 35 Corte Madera Avenue. Prior to this, Smith and Hawken was located for a brief time on Miller Avenue. The home-and-garden business was founded in 1979 by Paul Hawken, the visionary environmentalist who lived for a time in Mill Valley. In May 2006, a new, 10,000-square-foot store was opened in Strawberry. Some of the staff is pictured in front of the new store in 2007. (Both courtesy of Suki Hill.)

A bank has been located at the corner of Throckmorton and Corte Madera Avenues in downtown Mill Valley since 1911. In 1927, the Bank of Mill Valley, whose interior and small staff are shown in this photograph, was bought by the Liberty Bank of America. Shortly thereafter, this became the Bank of Italy and then changed its name to the Bank of America in 1930. The interior of the bank today is in sharp contrast to the 1927 photograph. It seems more spacious and quite busy with a number of employees. (Then courtesy of MVLHR; now courtesy of Suki Hill.)

Here are more partial views of Lytton Square, one taken in the 1940s, and the other in 2007. The original building on the corner of Throckmorton and Miller Avenues was built in 1906 and has housed a coffee business for a number of years under various ownerships. Prior to its coffee history, it was Mayer's Department Store until 1973. In the 1940s view from the same vantage point, one can see the Greyhound Bus Depot and Alberts, a department store until 1954. (Then courtesy of Jim Staley; now courtesy of Suki Hill.)

THROCKMORTON AVENUE, MILL VALLEY, CALIFORNIA   3505

Businesses occupying this building at 41 Throckmorton Avenue have always involved food. Pictured here in 1963 is Sonapa Farms, a restaurant and delicatessen that remained for several decades. In the late 1990s, it was briefly Sonapa Bistro, then Noah's Bagels, and now in 2007, the Champagne Bakery and Café. With Summerhouse as its neighbor and Maison Reve at 11 Throckmorton, the block has become the place for Francophiles. (Then courtesy of Madison Devlin; now courtesy of Suki Hill.)

A couple drives an "antique" British coupe convertible on Throckmorton near the corner of Bernard Street. The rest of the cars in the picture seem to be from the early 1940s. The Old Mill Tavern is on the corner, and one can see part of Lytton Square, Rutherford's Drugstore, and all the way to Corte Madera Avenue and the Green Frog Food Center (now the Mill Valley Market). On the same corner today, we have a glimpse of Vasco's Bar and Restaurant. The cars parked in front are both BMWs—still the preferred car for wealthy Marinites. (Then courtesy of MVLHR; now courtesy of Suki Hill.)

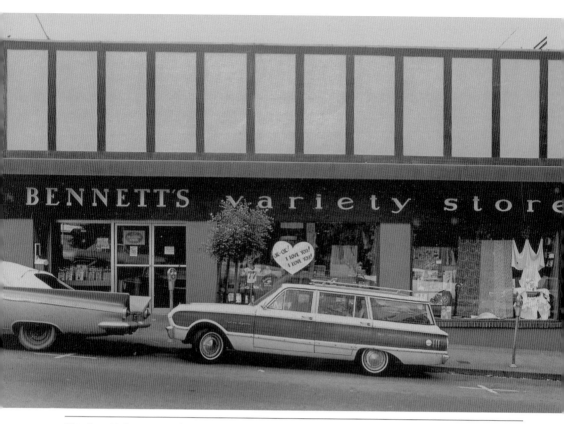

This late-1960s picture shows Bennett's Variety Store at 21 Throckmorton Avenue, a popular old-fashioned, no-frills variety store selling everything from sewing materials to hula hoops. Children could often be seen loitering on the corner and gathering to play sidewalk games—unheard of for young children in this day and age. In its place, established in the 1980s, is Summerhouse, a "shabby chic meets boho" type store and Tamalpais General Store, a high end gift store. (Then courtesy of Madison Devlin; now courtesy of Suki Hill.)

Varney's Hardware, located at 57 Throckmorton Avenue, was in business from 1933 to 1995. The Redwood Stables occupied this site from the 1890s to 1929. Pictured are Sam and Marie Schneider, who operated Varney's Hardware for many years. Now that Varney's Hardware is no longer, the building space is occupied by Wilkes Bashford, a breathtakingly (pocket-book wise) upscale clothing store. Some of the members of the staff pose outside the store in 2007. (Both courtesy of Suki Hill.)

The Emporium Department Store delivery wagon is parked in front of 116 Throckmorton Avenue, which housed the real estate office of the Tamalpais Land and Water Company in 1908. On the left is 118 Throckmorton Avenue, built in the 1890s and still standing today. Today 116 Throckmorton Avenue is the home of Lando's clothing store, and to the right, at 108, is Pullman and Company. (Then courtesy of MVLHR; now courtesy of Suki Hill.)

The old train depot became a Greyhound Bus terminal and taxi stand in 1940 and remained so until the early 1960s, when Greyhound no longer used the area. Temporarily the plaza area became a rather bleak parking lot, shown in this 1967 photograph. In 1982, the city-owned building was remodeled and became the Depot Bookstore and Café. Bricks were laid in the area, trees were planted, and soon the plaza became a pleasant gathering place for locals and tourists alike. (Both courtesy of Suki Hill.)

BANK OF MILL VALLEY
MILL VALLEY, CALIFORNIA.

The Bank of Mill Valley was originally at 154 Throckmorton and moved in 1911 to a newly completed building by Harvey Klyce at the corner of Throckmorton and Corte Madera Avenues. It is pictured here in 1911, before it was bought out in 1927 by the Bank of Italy, which eventually became Bank of America. The Bank of America remains in the same building today and appears much the same except for the addition of an automatic teller machine and the growth of trees, which hadn't been planted yet in 1911. (Then courtesy of Jim Staley; now courtesy of Suki Hill.)

BUSINESSES

The Wheeler Martin Pioneer Grocery Store, pictured in 1899, stood at 106 Throckmorton Avenue. Wheeler Martin, the proprietor, stands with his hands on his hips. The left window indicates that the store is "Agt. Log Cabin" (perhaps an agent to sell property?), and on the right that it sells Roberts Candy, cigars, and tobacco. There are brooms, hats, crockery, and baskets out front, and tins, jars, and a barrel in the window, along with a sign advertising pies for sale—a true emporium! This was the first lot sold in the 1890 auction of property in Mill Valley. It later became Allen and Roseveare, grocers. More recently, the building was occupied for many years by Old Mill Tavern. Currently it is Vasco's restaurant. (Then courtesy of MVLHR; now courtesy of Suki Hill.)

The Eastland Bakery was established in Mill Valley in 1893 and was the town's first bakery. In 1905, it moved to 14 Miller Avenue, where this photograph was taken. It remained a bakery with a number of different owners until 1960, when Lockwood's Pharmacy expanded into the site. Currently it is Margaret O'Leary, a fashionable clothing store. (Then courtesy of MVLHR; now courtesy of Suki Hill.)

In 1936, Esposti's soda fountain was remodeled to accommodate a restaurant. In 1944, Delemo and Kathleen Esposti became sole owners and operated the business until 1964, when they sold it to Sal and Maria Aversa, pictured here around 1980 with family in their restaurant, La Ginestra. Sal is on the left, wearing the chef's hat, his wife, Maria, is on the right, and their son Tino is next to Sal. This family-run restaurant now involves three generations of the Aversas and is very popular with local Mill Valley denizens. (Then courtesy of MVLHR; now courtesy of Suki Hill.)

This photograph, taken about 1935, looks down the west side of Miller Avenue. Up from the Eastland Bakery is the Wells Fargo Bank. Next is Young's Auto Dealership, then Tamalpais Hardware, and next a plumbing and appliance store. The building farthest on the left has been razed to create a vehicle passageway to a back parking lot. The small building next to it was also torn down in 1967 and rebuilt to house Valley Security and Tool, a locksmith shop that still operates there. The photograph taken in 2007 shows Wells Fargo Bank, which remains in its original location. But replacing the bakery is a children's store, beyond that a pet store, and at the corner a coffee shop. D'Angelos occupies the space where there was a car dealership, and next to D'Angelos is the dress shop Margaret O'Leary. Change is the nature of businesses on this block, and it reflects a shift from stores offering services to the community to tourism-oriented businesses. This is a trend that is inevitable in a community where the rents go up every year. (Then courtesy of Jim Staley; now courtesy of Suki Hill.)

The O'Shaughnessy Building was built in 1893 as the Mill Valley Hotel. Here, in the 1940s, it housed the Purity Market. On the corner was Red Hill Liquors, a business that remains there today. Next door was Varney Brothers Hardware Store. The 2007 photograph shows the Banana Republic store occupying the building, which was sold in the 1990s to Lee and Lum of San Francisco. The space is for lease, indicating that this branch of the large clothing chain, which opened its original store in Mill Valley in 1978, will soon be leaving the area. (Then courtesy of MVLHR; now courtesy of Suki Hill.)

Opened in 1912, this business was at the end of the Pipeline Trail and Mountain Railway's Muir Woods track. It changed hands in the 1950s but carried on the Swiss theme and name Mountain Home Inn, offering beer and bratwurst and catering to hikers, tourists, and the local community. In 1985, the Mountain Home Inn was renovated and became a rather upscale bed-and-breakfast inn while continuing the tradition of catering to the same clientele with their restaurant. The menu, however, became considerably more elaborate than the simple German fare served in its original incarnation. (Then courtesy of MVLHR; now courtesy of Suki Hill.)

These almost identical shots—one taken in 1967, and the other in 2007—are at 6 Locust Avenue in the Homestead area. The center building, partially obscured by a very long Cadillac, was at the former time a liquor store. If one looks carefully, two young men can be seen grinning from the door of what was the Brothers Tavern, a popular watering hole in the 1960s and 1970s. In the 2007 version, a large SUV obscures somewhat a barbershop that currently occupies this building. Next door is a bead shop called Beads of Marin. (Then courtesy of Madison Devlin; now courtesy of Suki Hill.)

An interior shot taken in 2000 shows the popular local watering hole the 2 AM Club. Formerly called the Brown Jug, "The Deuce" has been in this same spot since 1933. An interior shot features another bar in Jagtown, the Louvre, one of many saloons in the early 1900s that were beyond the jurisdiction of local officials and caused quite a stir because of their late hours and the occasional rowdy behavior of their patrons. Things are not so very different today, although the 2 AM Club, originally part of Homestead Valley, was annexed to the city in 1947 in order to curtail its hours of operation. The famous "toilet seat" guitar created by Charlie Deal still hangs behind the bar, as well as many amusing decorations. (Then courtesy of MVLHR; now courtesy of Suki Hill.)

CHAPTER

4

COMMUNITY
AND EVENTS

A young woman meditates in a spot near the top of the middle ridge overlooking Mill Valley. Three dogs congregate nearby. Possibly the most interesting and compelling aspects of Mill Valley are its people—its families, organizations, activities, and celebrations. The community of Mill Valley has always had a kind of integrity and free spirit that binds its citizens and allows for change. (Courtesy of Suki Hill.)

The Mill Valley Rotary Club poses at an annual meeting held in Muir Woods on May 24, 1938. These are approximately 50 men notably dressed in business suits at picnic tables laden with food for a luncheon. Also a point of interest in this photograph is the public telephone sign on the building behind. The modern photograph was taken in 1990 of the Rotary club luncheon meeting at the Golf Clubhouse on Buena Vista Avenue. (Then courtesy of MVLHR; now courtesy of Suki Hill.)

This *c.* 1907 photograph titled "Pioneer Ladies" is thought to be of some of the early members of the Outdoor Art Club. The Outdoor Art Club was founded in 1902 as a civic women's club. The purpose of the club was to preserve the natural scenery of Mill Valley and its surroundings and to beautify the grounds around public buildings. Taken in 2002, this photograph was commissioned by the Outdoor Art Club Board to commemorate the 100th anniversary of the club. (Then courtesy of MVLHR; now courtesy of Suki Hill.)

These young women are Mill Valley tourists, and they pose in front of the bus depot with their chaperone, *c.* 1940. Before the building became the Greyhound Bus Depot, it was the train station. In the photograph taken in 2007, the two young men stand in approximately the same spot in front of what is now the Book Depot and Café. They have crossed the Golden Gate Bridge on their bicycles and have purchased sandwiches and cold drinks. They happily pose for the photographer. (Both courtesy of Suki Hill.)

This early photograph seems to have been taken in downtown Mill Valley in the early 1920s. The young woman, with her hat, gloves, and Brownie camera, appears to be on her way to church on Sunday morning. In the modern photograph, taken in 2002, a young woman is going to her own kind of church: the beautiful outdoors of Mill Valley. Her modern-day Sunday attire includes a bike helmet, shoes, and a bottle of water. (Both courtesy of Suki Hill.)

Homestead residents got together a work party in 1905 and constructed a wooden sidewalk along Montford Avenue, from Miller Avenue (where this photograph was taken) to Ethel Avenue. The men, of all ages, including a young boy, pose here (approximately where the 2 AM Club is now) with their tools at their sides. The *c.* 1980 photograph shows a crew that worked on the development of the Flying Y Ranch, a mile or so up the way on Sequois Valley Road. They are shown here at the end of the day, beers in hand. The empty hill behind them, originally a ranch, now has a number of large homes on a street called Walsh Drive. (Both courtesy of Suki Hill.)

COMMUNITY AND EVENTS

Adorable young ladies pose for their picture perched on a countertop at the Mill Valley Bootery, which was located in downtown Mill Valley around 1918. Taken in the same area of Mill Valley as the Bootery had been, the current photograph displays sophisticated, charming modern-day shop girls. (Then courtesy of MVLHR; now courtesy of Suki Hill.)

These sporty young women are posing at Muir Beach around 1925. Their beachwear is interesting because it marks a time when bathing suits were no longer required to cover almost the entire body. For over a century, Muir Beach has been a popular recreation spot. Young surfers pose with their surfboards in the 1980s. Muir Beach is still a wonderful beach for swimming and picnicking, and it is often surfed by local novices. (Both courtesy of Suki Hill.)

With Mount Tamalpais in the background, a family portrait was taken in 1972 of new "hippie" parents. This photograph represents the iconic nature of residents who lived in Mill Valley in the 1960s and 1970s. In 2007, a baby girl, her parents, and their Labrador dog pose for their first family portrait. This handsome couple represents many of the young families that now live in Mill Valley and are a stark contrast to the "hippie" family in 1970. (Both courtesy of Suki Hill.)

In 1969, this young couple personally packs up their Jeep with their belongings from a home they were renting on Montford Avenue to make a move to their new home in another location on the mountain. As the wealth of Mill Valley residents has increased, so has the number of their belongings. In 2006, a huge moving van is backed up into a driveway on Molino to move the residents who have just sold their house. (Both courtesy of Suki Hill.)

Pictured here are members of the LaVerne baseball team in 1913. They appear to be happy, rough-and-tumble members of the team. In this time period, the members are quite formally dressed, especially the coach, who is in a suit. In 1984, the group is gathered in matching uniforms, while their coach is casually dressed. (Then courtesy of MVLHR; now courtesy of Suki Hill.)

Around the 1890s, the Coffin family (a distinguished early Mill Valley family) and friends gather around a picnic table in Old Mill Park. The rather formal attire and white table cloth on the picnic table contrast with the casual attire and less formal manner of the group photographed in 1999. The contemporary group is made up of numerous families celebrating Mother's Day in the park. (Then courtesy of MVLHR; now courtesy of Suki Hill.)

COMMUNITY AND EVENTS

A lovely photograph taken *c.* 1930 shows a small child with a walking stick just her size and two unidentified men. The caption on the photograph says: "The famous Pipeline Trail to Mount Tamalpais and Muir Woods National Park." The "Pipeline" in 2007 is still a gateway to the many trails on the mountain and a favorite thoroughfare for mountain bikers as well as runners and hikers. (Then courtesy of Jim Staley; now courtesy of Suki Hill.)

The famous "Pipe line Trail" to Mt. Tamalpais and Muir Woods National Park Mill Valley, Calif.

Emma Reimann, running in 1921 in the "Woman's Hike," had the winning time of 1:16:05. She received a silver cup and a pearl necklace for her victory. In 1922, she ran and won the race again with a record time of 1:12:06. This record time was not beaten until 1969. Note the young woman's attire. This picture of author Suki Hill was taken in 1969 in a location close to where Emma Reimann ran in 1921. All similarities end there. In all the 20 races the author participated in, her time was never much faster than 1:45:00. (Then courtesy of MVLHR; now courtesy of Suki Hill.)

Taken in 1920, this image shows participants at the third annual "Woman's Hike," now known as the Dipsea Race. The women's competition was called a hike to escape the Amateur Athletic Union (AAU) ban on long distance races for women. The women in this photograph are beginning to shed the required long skirts in place of more comfortable bloomer-type attire. In 2000, four female runners are lined up at the start line. Their skimpy attire is in contrast to what was worn by the women runners in 1920. Also noticeable is the combination of men and women in this handicapped race. Gender is no longer a factor, only age. (Then courtesy of Ted Wurm; now courtesy of Suki Hill.)

A group of young women pose in front of Old Mill School, obviously on some sort of outing. All have hats and fur stoles, apparently dressed for a celebration, perhaps a lady's tea or a bridal shower. Years later, another group of women gathers on a celebratory hike honoring a recently engaged member of the group. The attire reflects a modern-day "sporty" nature and an awareness of harsh sun exposure, as many members hold or wear hats and sunglasses and most carry water bottles. (Then courtesy of MVLHR; now courtesy of Suki Hill.)

COMMUNITY AND EVENTS

At the beginning of the Dipsea Race in 1946, one can see the Green Frog Market and the Old Mill Tavern in the background. Only 38 runners signed up for the race that year, as World War II had just ended. The Dipsea Race in 1969 shows an increase in participation compared to the previous photograph. The race is so popular that people from all over the country scramble to be admitted, and participation is now limited to 1,500. (Then courtesy of MVLHR; now courtesy of Suki Hill.)

The Mountain Play, so called because of its location on Mount Tamalpais, had its first performance in 1913. The natural amphitheater at the meadow and slope by Rock Springs was first envisioned by, among others, Austin Pohli, whose parents summered at 41 Bigelow Avenue in Mill Valley (the house is still standing) in the mid-1890s. In this late-1940s picture, playgoers are seated on the grassy slopes. Some 1,200 people attended the first Mountain Play, and it was deemed a grand success. The photograph from the late 1990s shows a considerably larger crowd; perhaps as many as 10,000 people attended this performance. (Then courtesy of MVLHR; now courtesy of Suki Hill.)

Courtesy of the Lucretia Little History Room, Mill Valley Public Library

The original Our Lady of Mount Carmel Catholic Church was built on Summit Avenue in 1893 and rather quickly became overcrowded. The new church, pictured here, was built in 1916 on Buena Vista Street at Oakdale Avenue and lasted until it too became too small for the growing congregation. The church was demolished in 1956, and while plans were being made for a newer, larger church, services were held in the parochial school auditorium for 12 years. Today's 12-sided church with its 136-foot spire was completed in 1968. (Then courtesy of Jim Staley; now courtesy of Suki Hill.)

Old Mill School with Mt Tamalpais in the distance - Mill Valley, Calif.

Old Mill School, originally the site of a mineral spring, opened officially in 1921. The sulfur spring beneath the asphalt playground at the rear of the school continued to bubble up as late as 1996, when the school playground was renovated. In this *c.* 1945 photograph, one can see children with crossing guard uniforms and there is a good view of Mount Tamalpais. The other photograph is from the identical vantage point in 2007. Mount Tamalpais is nearly obscured by trees and the school nearly obscured by an icon of the early 21st century, a sport utility vehicle. (Then courtesy of Jim Staley; now courtesy of Suki Hill.)

COMMUNITY AND EVENTS

The innocence and charm of these Tamalpais High School students celebrating "Class Day" in 1914 is in sharp contrast to the graduates of Tamalpais High School in 1998. Althought the graduates all are dressed in cap and gown, there is a kind of raucous exuberance that would have probably been unseemly in 1914. (Then courtesy of MVLHR; now courtesy of Suki Hill.)

The Mill Valley Fire Station was built in 1908 on Corte Madera Avenue. This building was a two-story, 20-by-50-foot wood structure. The upstairs of the original building was used as Mill Valley's first town hall. In 2007, members of the Mill Valley Fire Department pose for a picture in front of the fire station, still located on Corte Madera Avenue. The fire station is located adjacent to city hall, which was built in 1936. (Then courtesy of MVLHR; now courtesy of Suki Hill.)

Members of the Mill Valley police force pose in front of city hall around 1940. In 1990, three members of the force, including officer Ed Johnson (center), a motorcycle policeman famous because he probably gave tickets to half of Mill Valley's residents during his long tenure. They stand in front of Bill's Fixatorium, which was demolished to make way for low-cost housing. (Then courtesy of MVLHR; now courtesy of Suki Hill.)

In 1968, the Mill Valley City Council unanimously approved a resolution calling for the immediate withdrawal of American troops from Vietnam. Students from Tamalpais High School were ardent supporters of this resolution and were an active and vocal part of the community. In July 2007, this photograph of peace demonstrators, many from the Redwoods Retirement Center, rallied to end the United States' war in Iraq. (Both courtesy of Suki Hill.)

Mill Valley's Congregational Church dates back to 1897, but the church that still stands (pictured here in 2007) was originally built in 1930, the design inspired by a drawing of the Maybeck-designed Outdoor Art Club. This *c.* 1935 photograph does not include the additional buildings created with the purchase of several more lots on Olive Street, expanding the church's facilities for its ever-expanding congregation. (Then courtesy of Jim Staley; now courtesy of Suki Hill.)

Community Church
Mill Valley, Calif.

DISCOVER THOUSANDS OF LOCAL HISTORY BOOKS
FEATURING MILLIONS OF VINTAGE IMAGES

Arcadia Publishing, the leading local history publisher in the United States, is committed to making history accessible and meaningful through publishing books that celebrate and preserve the heritage of America's people and places.

Find more books like this at
www.arcadiapublishing.com

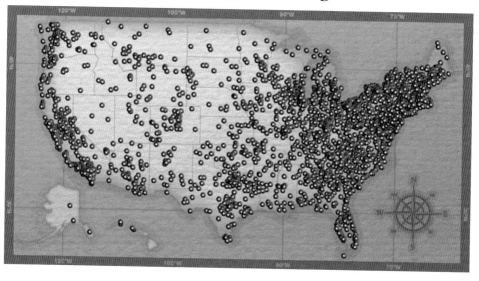

Search for your hometown history, your old stomping grounds, and even your favorite sports team.